Non-executive Directors

A BDO Stoy Hayward Guide for Growing Businesses

Rupert Merson

PROFILE BOOKS

First published in Great Britain in 2003 by
PROFILE BOOKS LTD
58A Hatton Garden
London EC1N 8LX
www.profilebooks.co.uk

A CIP catalogue record for this book is available from the British Library.

ISBN 1 86197 499 X

Typeset in Galliard by MacGuru Ltd
info@macguru.org.uk

Printed in Great Britain by
Bookmarque, Croydon, Surrey

While care has been taken to ensure the accuracy of the contents of this book,
it is intended to provide general guidance only and does not constitute
professional advice.

To Jo, Lucy, Oliver, Barnaby and Wilf

'What is the use of a book,' thought Alice,
'without pictures or conversations?'

Contents

Foreword

I COME ACROSS OWNER-MANAGERS of businesses big and small at Cranfield: increasingly they are interested in the advantage to be gained from having a decent non-executive who really understands the needs of a growing, entrepreneurial business. Yet in all the reams of advice devoted to the role of non-executive directors, some of it credible and thoughtful, rather more of it turgid and obscure, almost nothing has been written about that role in the type of business that has the greatest need of help and advice.

Growing owner-managed businesses, the lifeblood of any economy, are all too often dismissed in the occasional all-embracing sentence or two. So Rupert Merson's book is to be welcomed as the first to concentrate on this all-important sector. Written in an informal and accessible style well judged for its audience, it is nevertheless rigorously researched and has the authoritative tone of a seasoned practitioner.

Whether looking for a non-executive director for the first time, or trying to get more value from the ones already in place, every owner-manager will find this book an invaluable guide. It – along with the others in this BDO series – comes at the right time and meets a real need.

COLIN BARROW
Head of the Enterprise Group
Cranfield School of Management
June 2003

1

Introduction

THIS IS ONE in a series of short books on the key roles in growing, owner-managed businesses. The first one was about the finance director. This one is about the role of the non-executive director.

Readers who raised one eyebrow at starting a series with the finance director will no doubt raise both when they see the role of the non-executive director given higher priority than some of the other roles in the top management team. And, to be fair, the role of the 'non-exec' has come in for a pasting recently. Lord Young of Graffham, former Secretary of State for Trade and Industry under Margaret Thatcher and ex-chairman of Cable and Wireless, announced as he was leaving his post of President of the Institute of Directors that the non-exec should be done away with altogether. All directors should become full-time and executive, leaving independent scrutiny to shareholders. It was 'dangerous nonsense', he said, to assume that part-time non-executives could know enough about what was going on to spot problems. Lord Young's views are controversial. Certainly the Institute of Directors has sought to distance itself from them. The incoming president, presumably speaking in an official

'The victim-hunters in and around Enron, recovering from the joys of taking down Andersen, are seeking fresh meat.'

capacity, said, 'Lord Young is speaking in a personal capacity and his views do not reflect the policy of the Institute.'[1]

But Lord Young is not the only doubter. Although Lord Young was not Cable & Wireless's chairman at the time, it is ironic that Cable & Wireless's plummeting share price in the autumn of 2002 was accompanied by a chorus of newspaper criticism about the role of the company's non-execs. In another context, Tiny Rowland, former head of Lonrho, famously noted that non-execs were 'about as

much use as Christmas tree decorations'. For other observers, the role of non-exec, rather than being merely decorative, has become simply too risky. The victim-hunters in and around Enron, recovering from the joys of taking down Andersen, are seeking fresh meat. The financiers are one target. The directors are another. Indeed, the role of director is under scrutiny as never before. The Sarbanes-Oxley legislation in the USA (President Bush's 2002 Act 'to protect investors by improving the accuracy and reliability of corporate disclosures') is a case in point. Some of the penalties under the legislation for misdemeanours committed by directors of listed companies are more severe than penalties for many violent crimes. A fraud conviction relating to the purchase or sale of shares can earn a director a 20-year prison term. A CEO or CFO who falsely certifies a company's financial statements can get ten years in prison and a $1 million fine. But whilst those actively and directly involved in the execution of financial skulduggery – the executive directors – may have something to answer for, non-execs may wonder whether they should be labelled as villains or as victims of circumstances beyond their control. Did they really know what was going on? And even if they were supposed to know, were they really *able* to know? And, either way, who in their right minds would want to carry the risk? The non-exec may have a key role to play in reducing corporate risk – but if reducing corporate risk means converting it to personal risk, many can be forgiven for questioning whether this is a sensible thing to do.

The focus of this series of books is on the owner-managed business with ambitions to grow. Whereas much attention has been paid to the problems of the role of non-executive in the listed business, the role of non-exec in the private business has been largely ignored, or tarred with the same brush. Derek Higgs, commenting on draft recommendations on the role of non-execs, said, 'I do not presume that a one-size-fits-all approach to governance is appropriate.'[2] The Higgs report was only aimed at listed companies. 'Smaller listed companies' are specially treated to two pages out of a total of 126, and non-listed companies are offered only the 'hope that the review will be of wider interest and use'. Of course Higgs cannot be blamed for the issue he was asked to address, which was corporate governance in the UK listed sector. But there remains a failure to explore properly the relevance of the role of non-exec in the smaller business. Worse still, there often seems to be a cavalier assumption on the part of those reporting Higgs that it's *all* non-executives he's referring to, rather than just those in listed businesses.

But the issue is more fundamental than one of being misrepresented or misunderstood by the press. Most agree that non-execs have a part to play in big PLCs – but does a non-exec have *anything* to offer the smaller, owner-managed business? Research would seem to show that there is a good corollary between company size and its enthusiasm for non-execs. One study for the Association of Chartered Certified Accountants suggests that the majority of small and medium-sized enterprises (SMEs) don't have a non-exec at all – and the proportion falls to as few as one in five for those businesses with fewer than 50 staff. [3] Nor can the same study find any connection between having a non-exec and improved financial performance – hardly a ringing endorsement.

Yet a key argument in this book is that the non-executive does indeed have an important part to play in the owner-managed business with ambitions to grow, and that this contribution does not fly in the face of common sense or recent experience, but is based on a thorough understanding of how these businesses work and what they need. Indeed, in large part this book benefits from conversations with many such non-execs in private businesses, all of whom have been generous with their experiences and insights.

Another theme of this series of books is that it is a mistake to assume that what is needed by big listed business is needed by owner-managed business. The role of non-exec in the latter may share some of the same elements as the role of non-exec in those businesses that make the headlines, but the way those elements are put together and the overall nature of the role in some ways are quite different. In the next few pages we will explore the role in more detail, drawing on the real experiences of those who have made smaller businesses their lives' work, pointing out the parallels and the differences with the role in big business.

This book aims to be a help and a guide rather than a piece of polemic arguing a case for the non-exec in the owner-managed business. But if it encourages a few more owner-managed businesses to recruit a non-exec I think that will be a step forward.

- ▪ Only the minority of owner-managed businesses have non-executive directors
- ▪ The role of non-exec has come under increasing scrutiny recently – but the interests of big listed companies have attracted almost all of the attention
- ▪ The role a non-exec plays in a non-listed business can be substantially different from that played in a big business – but is important nonetheless

2

What a non-executive director is

WE NEED TO BREAK THIS DOWN into its constituent parts.
What makes a director non-executive? And what is different
about being a non-exec to an owner-managed business?

Non-executives and executives

If you're wondering exactly what a non-executive director is,
don't expect to get much help from the law. Apparently it's
one of the most important functions within any company, but
although statute refers to directors, it does not distinguish
between the executive and non-executive kinds. Company law
starts from the basis that all directors are equal, at least in
terms of responsibility. Such limited differences as there are
arise from case law and current practice.

So what is the difference between a non-exec and an executive? It is too easy to draw up lists of contrasting characteristics that define the executive and the non-executive as
follows:

Executive	*Non-executive*
Hands-on	Hands-off
Not independent	Independent
Full-time	Part-time
Employed	Self-employed
Strategist	Policeman
Internal knowledge	External knowledge

Unfortunately, reality cannot be tidily reduced to mutually exclusive lists such as these. When defining the difference

> **'When I think of the relationship** between the executive and the non-executive, I often think of Alice's conversation with the Cheshire Cat:
>
> *Just then Alice noticed the Cheshire-Cat sitting in a tree nearby. It saw Alice and grinned.*
>
> *"Cheshire-Cat," said Alice, "please could you tell me which way I should go?"*
>
> *"That depends on where you want to go," the Cheshire-Cat answered.*
>
> *"I don't really care," said Alice.*
>
> *"Well it doesn't matter then, does it?" the Cheshire-Cat said.*
>
> The non-exec has a key role in helping the executive realise his ambitions – but the exec has to have the ambitions, and some idea of where he wants to go.'

between non-execs and executives we need to talk of tendencies, not absolutes – shades of grey, rather than black and white. It is perhaps because of this that statute has fought shy of coming up with a definition itself. Treated as tendencies, the terms in the above lists become much more useful. We'll consider each of them in turn.

It is fair to observe that non-executive directors tend not to be involved with day-to-day management. In the past, 'hands-off' has led to the title 'non-executive director' signifying a big name who adorns a company letterhead, turns up for the sherry after the meeting, and treats the meeting itself as a rest before the sherry. Even if larger companies were once amenable, smaller, owner-managed companies, unsurprisingly, have never had much time for this sort of thing (and big names have never had much time for smaller companies). In the current business world, 'hands-off' for the non-exec suggests someone who is not encumbered with specific management responsibility. There will be no reporting lines into a non-exec – dotted or otherwise. However, 'hands-off' cannot be taken too far. Non-execs never were formally absolved from management responsibility. They are and always were part of the board and, whilst the actual mechanics of day-to-day management may well be an executive responsibility, ultimate responsibility for the management is shared with the non-executives. In a smaller, owner-managed business, active involvement of the non-executive in day-to-day management is far more likely – indeed, many small businesses would find it difficult to countenance recruiting a non-exec who wasn't prepared to get dirt under his fingernails. 'Hands-off' in the small business often means little more than 'without portfolio', or not specifically responsible for any one part of the business more than another – but not afraid of interfering where necessary.

'Independent' is often used as an alternative term to 'non-executive' – or perhaps to describe the key quality that many

'We need to break this down into its constituent parts. What makes a director non-executive? And what is different about being a non-exec of a smaller business?'

would like their non-executives to possess. Non-execs are usually associated with independence when internal corporate governance and policing roles are being discussed. Indeed, being *seen* to be independent in this context is perhaps even more important than *being* independent. But again the label 'independent' describes a tendency. The fact that the London Stock Exchange's 'Combined Code' requires the majority of non-execs to be independent as well as non-executive suggests how little the two terms have to do with each other in reality. As has been frequently observed, all independent directors are non-executive, but not all non-executives are independent. Any mention of the term 'independent' immediately begs a question: independent of whom? Some entrepreneurial businesses, for example, have non-execs imposed on them by venture capitalists. Such directors are 'independent' of the company, but they are nevertheless not truly independent. Indeed, their role is primarily to safeguard the interests of the venture capitalist, which often clash with those of the company.

Independence itself is a quality that is difficult to pin down, and surprisingly difficult to define. Take the board of Apple, for example. This board, although directing a big business, has characteristics that many smaller businesses will find all too familiar. It has only five members in addition to the CEO. Of these, one, though nominally independent under US guidelines, and the chair of the company's audit committee, formerly worked at Apple, and sold his own software business to Apple.[4]

The following characteristics (some of which are discussed later) are indicative of a state of independence:

- The individual hasn't been employed by the company recently, and thus is not predisposed either for or against some parts of the business.
- The individual is not a retained professional adviser, and thus not influenced either by his fee or by judgements taken by another organisation in which he has an interest.

'Independence in this sense is a personal attribute.'

- The individual is not a supplier or customer of the company, and thus not likely to influence the company towards or away from one contract or another – although it should be noted that many non-execs will be expected to have industry expertise.
- The individual does not have a family connection with someone in the business.
- The individual's directorship is for a fixed term, and he is less likely to be motivated by self-preservation when taking decisions.
- The individual does not depend so heavily on his remuneration from the company as to make resignation difficult. The ability – and willingness – to resign is the ultimate test of independence. Unsurprisingly, recommendations and guidelines that have emanated

from the various corporate governance reviews in recent years almost always include the obligatory resignation of the non-executives after a specified period of years. An interesting demonstration of failure to display this characteristic is the non-exec who makes a seat on the board a condition of his investment. Such an individual is hardly likely to agree to his own compulsory resignation. But then, as noted above, neither is he really to be thought of as independent. A non-exec with share options might also be argued to have compromised his independence in this regard.

Once again this context seems to be more relevant to non-execs in big, listed businesses, subject to the scrutiny of an

> **'Independence is critical** for the non-exec in the smaller business – but a non-exec will only be independent if the executives – the owner-managers – *let* him be independent and *want* him to be independent.'

array of outside interests, including, of course, shareholders. But independence is also an important quality for non-execs in private businesses, for whom corporate governance and acting as the eyes and ears of the shareholder may be less of an issue. For a non-exec to support the management team of the owner-managed business, he has to have a greater degree of independence from it than the executives – an ability to step back and see the wood from the trees, and a more detached commitment to the business than that expected of executives,

'Perhaps the most important trade-off is between "strategist" and "policeman".'

who on occasion can get a little over-excited. What matters in the private business is independence of mind rather than independence defined in terms of relationships and financial interests. Independence in this sense is a personal attribute, and it is more valuable to the private company than independence in the listed company sense. Indeed, independence in the listed company sense is often almost an irrelevance in the private business that is 100 per cent owned by one or two shareholders. Independence of mind, on the other hand, is priceless.

Almost all non-exec positions are part-time. But here again the 'tendency' rule still applies. Certainly, at times of crisis, or times when the non-execs are under particular pressure (such as when recruiting a new CEO, for example), the role of non-exec may well seem full-time. But the fact that recent recommendations suggest limiting the number of non-exec positions in listed businesses held by any one individual to five suggests that part-time is the expectation. If no individual is expected to hold more than five non-exec positions, this implies that a non-exec might spend up to a day a week on each directorship. In my experience, a day a week sounds rather a lot for a non-exec involved in a small business. True, at the beginning of an appointment it's likely to be much more – there are people to meet and documents to read. And, once established, the work will still involve much more than merely attending board meetings. You can do your sums for yourself – although the Association of Chartered Certified Accountants' study on the role of non-execs reports that the average amount of time non-execs spend working with 'small and medium-sized enterprises' is just eighteen days a year.

The question of whether or not the role of non-exec is a form of employment is one that is complicated by employment law and tax law, which, as so often, have the effect of clouding the issue rather than clarifying it. Tax law has increasingly tended to see employment relationships where there aren't any. But, as a matter of fact even if not as a matter of tax law, the non-exec role tends to be that of an outsider looking in rather than that of an inside employee. Indeed, whereas many if not most executives will have service contracts as employees to back up their appointments as directors, the majority of non-execs will not, relying on letters of appointment, and, in some cases, consultancy agreements only. The tax aspects of appointing a non-exec are discussed in more detail in the 'Useful information' chapter at the end of this book.

When discussing what a non-exec is in terms of 'tendencies', perhaps the most important trade-off is between 'strategist' and 'policeman' – the role of setting and implementing corporate strategy, and the role of acting as watchdog and whistleblower for the outside world, ensuring adherence to good practice, respect for the interests of other stakeholders, adherence to the processes of boardroom discipline, and so on. If the role of strategist is usually associated with that of the executive, the role of policeman is associated with that of the non-executive. But of course the two roles are not mutually exclusive.

The non-executive director's role is well explored in the Cadbury Committee and the Hampel Review – albeit principally with the big business in mind. The Cadbury Committee tended to stress the corporate governance and 'policeman' benefits of a strong non-executive representation on a board, whereas the Hampel Review also emphasised the strategic thinking that non-executives can bring. Higgs notes that 'Non-executive directors are the custodians of the governance process.' But Higgs is also at pains to stress that the two roles should be seen as complementary rather than conflicting. He also rightly hints that the excitement about the monitoring role perhaps owes something to the views of US regulators, 'who have tended to emphasise the monitoring role at the possible expense of the contribution the non-executive director can make to wealth creation'. For Higgs, an 'overemphasis on monitoring' will alienate a non-exec from the rest of the board. On the other hand, an 'overemphasis on strategy' risks undermining governance. Nevertheless, the corporate governance and accountability aspects of a board's performance should be a key role of the non-exec in a company with external stakeholders – typically, therefore, a larger, publicly quoted company. This part of the role includes, *inter alia*: ensuring due process is followed, e.g. in relation to auditors, conflicts of interest and so on; ensuring the interests of non-board stakeholders are considered; and reviewing executive pay, performance and succession. More details of this part of the role are discussed in the next chapter.

Owner-managed businesses may not have to worry so much about external stakeholders, but nevertheless there will still be some stakeholders, and they will want to see that the company they do business with ensures their interests are appropriately dealt with. The policing role therefore implies an influence on strategy – indeed, if it isn't interwoven into strategy delivery, the policing role is likely to be more honoured in the breach than in the observance. However, it's to be expected that non-execs will have a more direct influence on strategy on the boards of privately owned companies than on the boards of listed companies. The ways in which non-execs exercise this influence will vary. The non-exec is unlikely to deliver by exercising entrepreneurial qualities, but he will be expected to challenge the thinking of the executive directors and bring commercial skills and experience to the decision-making process. The truth is that if non-execs don't have a strategic role, in the smaller business they won't add value. And if they don't add value, they won't have a role at all.

The last executive/non-executive 'tendency' is the one that

explores the tension between internal knowledge and external knowledge. Again, the area is both grey and contentious. As a part-timer with less experience of the business than the executives, a non-exec will therefore also have far less knowledge of its internal workings. On the other hand, a good non-exec will be able to bring to the board an awareness of the external context that will both compensate for his relative lack of knowledge of what is going on inside and enhance the overall capabilities of the board. However, it must be remembered that the non-exec is a director and is responsible for the business. Being non-exec is an explanation, but not an acceptable reason, for ignorance.

Non-executives and advisers

If you can define a non-exec with reference to an executive, you can do the same with reference to the bevy of professional advisers – lawyers, accountants, bankers, surveyors and so on – all of whom seem to have been keen in recent years to offer non-exec-style advice to the boards of companies. For the 'policeman' role, you can turn to your lawyer or your auditor. As for the 'strategist' role, everyone seems to offer that. So why bother with a non-exec at all?

To start with, although good non-execs are often held out by executives as great providers of 'advice', the non-exec role is much bigger than the role of adviser. The non-exec is a director, and shares the legal duties and responsibilities of the executive directors. An adviser has a different relationship with the business. For one thing, she doesn't have the same legal worries. She won't have to worry about being barred if the company trades whilst insolvent, nor will she risk criminal prosecution if the business falls seriously foul of health and safety legislation. When backs are against the wall, it will become clear which business the adviser is really committed to – and it will be her own, not her client's. Indeed, many professional advisers are scrupulous, if not paranoid on some occasions, about ensuring they don't fall into the 'trap' of

> **'I have to keep reminding** the board that the role of advisers is to advise: our role as directors is to decide.'

being seen as 'shadow directors' – i.e. being considered to be directors in law because they have actually been acting as directors in fact. I was given an insight into the other side of this when I once asked a contact of mine, retiring from executive responsibilities, whether he'd be interested in any non-executive roles that came my way, and he told me that he really didn't want 'all the hassle' of being a non-exec. If I had any *consultancy* assignments for him – now that would be different.

Advisers also differ from non-execs in their relation to independence – and it is the adviser rather than the non-exec who often has a problem with independence. This may at first seem paradoxical, but, although all advisers have a duty to their clients, most advisers owe principal loyalty to the organisations they are employed by and on behalf of which they are providing advice. A truly independent non-exec is acting on his own behalf. Many business people know the frustration of trying to get advisers to 'say what they really think'. Getting an adviser to climb off the fence is compromised by the fact that there is a fee involved, and a relationship between two organisations to preserve, and by the adviser's determination to be loyal to the service line that her firm sells. The last key difference is that when the assignment is finished, the adviser walks away. The very fact that most consultants and advisers endlessly stress that they handhold their clients through implementation exposes their sensitivity on this point. For the non-exec, the only form of walking away is resignation. If his recommendations are not followed, the non-exec has to judge whether this is a matter that calls into question his director-ship – a far more serious matter than an adviser's disappoint-ment about not earning more fees from helping with implementation.

There is thus a clear distinction between being a non-exec, and being an adviser. The fact that many non-execs also act as 'consultants' should not be allowed to cloud this distinction. An individual with both hats should know, and his board should know, which hat he is wearing and when, and how he is being paid.

Non-executives and mentors

There is perhaps another important distinction to be made.

Many non-execs will recognise that they have a role in mentoring the chief executives of the businesses they work with. And non-execs to small businesses are more likely to recognise this than are non-execs to big businesses. The younger, less experienced entrepreneur is more likely to need the sort of personal support that a mentor can bring. Being an entrepreneur can be a lonely existence, and many appreciate the personal support and advice that a good non-executive can provide.

But there is an important difference between the role of mentor and the role of director. At its core, a mentoring relationship is very personal. A good relationship will involve much discussion that will not and should not reach anyone else's ears. For a mentor to be able to discuss development needs and concerns, there has to be absolute trust and understanding between mentor and mentoree.

A non-executive director, on the other hand – despite the importance of personal trust between board members – will never be, and should never be, as close as a mentor to any member of the board. A non-exec should never forget that he is part of the board, not outside it. He shares in a collective responsibility, and his loyalty to the board as a whole should

---

- Defining what a non-exec is can be difficult. There isn't even a definition in company statute
- The non-exec role may be defined by contrasting it with the roles of executive, adviser and mentor – elements of which are also part of the non-exec role
- A key quality is independence – but even this isn't absolute in the real world
- There are many influences that can affect a director's independence: factions and departments in the business, a client or customer, a supplier, a financier, a personal financial interest, remuneration, past experience in the business

be greater than any sense of loyalty to, or shared confidence with, any one member of it. Put another way, being independent means being independent of the CEO or anyone else in the company, as well as independent of the company itself and any outside interest. Of course, there is a lot of grey in this area of 'what it is to be a non-exec' – and a good non-exec will need to exercise judgement in deciding when to offer counsel and on what. But non-execs should never forget that, in spite of all the grey, some issues are straightforwardly black-and-white. Failing to recognise them as such and act accordingly in the best interests of the company would be to invite censure. It would also demonstrate a failure to understand what being a non-exec is all about.

3

What a non-executive director does

'THE NON-EXEC WHO HAD TO DO SOMETHING' sounds a bit like an old joke. But the relatively inactive non-exec appears to have continued to be a reality until quite recently. Sir Roger Hurn, ex-chairman of Marconi (and also chairman of Prudential), was quoted after the Marconi debacle as praising his non-executive directors for being 'extremely diligent in turning up' – as if they had no function other than to turn up and (perhaps) pay attention.[5]

Things have changed – even for Marconi. In the post-Enron, post-Worldcom world, non-executive directors and executive directors in big, listed businesses are aware of

---

'A non-exec is like a bidet: no one knows what he does, but he adds a bit of class.' [attributed to Michael Grade]

---

having duties they might not have paid attention to previously. The duties of directors of listed companies involve ensuring that existing processes for reviewing the effectiveness of financial controls are extended to include operational and compliance controls. Non-execs are not absolved from this responsibility – and arguably, as the eyes and ears of the shareholders, they have an extra responsibility for managing and monitoring controls that ensure the directors perform these duties.

The role of corporate policeman referred to in the last chapter manifests itself in particular tasks identified by the guidelines. The London Stock Exchange's Combined Code indicates that the audit committee and remuneration committee of listed companies should consist entirely of non-execs and the nomination committee (for appointing senior executives) should be controlled by non-execs. In addition the code indicates that at least a third of board members should be non-execs. Higgs wants at least half to be independent. The expectation is also nowadays that at the very least the role of chief executive and chairman will be split, and many would counsel that the interests of all are best served if the chairman of the board is non-executive, thus ensuring that the board itself fulfils its responsibilities by separating board management from company management. Indeed, Higgs recommends that the revised code should clearly state that the roles should be split – suggesting that this is a key strength of the UK corporate governance framework when contrasted with the US approach, where only a fifth of listed companies separate the roles. Higgs also recommends that at the time of appointment, the chairman should be 'independent'.

So much for the big, listed PLC. But what about the owner-managed, entrepreneurial business with ambition to grow? All of the tasks summarised above as being typical of the role of the non-executive in the listed business may be translated into tasks that need to be performed in the owner-managed business as follows.

Acting in the interests of the shareholder?

Much focus has fallen recently on the role of the non-exec as steward of the interests of the shareholder. The assumption is that in a listed business there are occasions when the executive team is under pressure to forget who really owns the business and to whom the directors are ultimately accountable. But in the private, entrepreneurial business – the owner-managed business – the directors often are the owners. Surely, even in

> **As a consequence of a change of policy** at their venture capitalist, one private company was requested to take on a non-exec in a governance role. The company refused, arguing that the 'policeman' role was unconstructive.

today's increasingly litigious world, the executives do not need protecting from themselves? Maybe not, but many leaders of young businesses nevertheless occasionally confuse their roles as directors with their roles as shareholders. Directors of owner-managed businesses, far from paying insufficient attention to their responsibility to shareholders, often fail to separate shareholder issues from operational issues and allow the former to get in the way of the latter. An experienced non-exec will help an inexperienced management team ensure that shareholder issues and operational issues are discussed separately, using separate processes. Furthermore, as the company

'Much focus has recently fallen on the role of the non-exec as steward of the interests of the shareholder.'

grows and the number of stakeholders increases, the executive team will rely on the non-executives more and more for ensuring that board processes evolve to reflect the issues and points of view that need to be tabled. Too many private businesses pay insufficient attention to the interests, for example, of minority shareholders who do not have board representation.

Audit committee?

No corporate governance issue has been the subject of greater attention recently than the relationship between a listed company and its auditors. The audit committee – a committee of the board, often comprised entirely of non-execs – is supposed to be an independent vehicle for managing the relationship, ensuring that the external auditors do their job effectively, rigorously and efficiently, and ensuring that internal audit processes are sufficiently strong and recommendations acted on. Most smaller businesses, however, are less likely to have internal audit departments. Some of the smallest will not even be required statutorily to have an external audit. Does this mean that another key non-exec task does not apply to the smaller business? Not really, no. For many smaller businesses, a non-exec is the closest they will get to having an internal auditor, and the small size of the business doesn't mean it will not benefit from an independent eye, critically reviewing processes and controls. Similarly, even if the business isn't of a size to need a statutory external audit, there are stakeholders who will be keen to see the existence of external reviews and controls. The presence of a competent non-executive will give comfort to potential suppliers and bankers, for example.

Remuneration committee?

Most people have to rely on their bosses to determine their

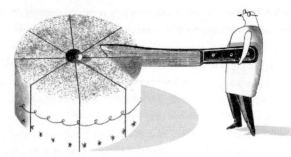

'Few issues are as divisive in the owner-managed business as the remuneration of members of the top team.'

salary rises. But if you are the boss, you have a splendid opportunity for abusing your own position. And if your business is funded by independent shareholders, then you will be funding your decisions to your benefit at their expense. It is unsurprising, therefore, that a key non-exec role in the listed business involves sitting on the remuneration committee and

'There's always likely to be a conflict. So the non-execs determine the remuneration of the execs: but at the end of the day, don't forget who really appointed the non-execs ...'

ensuring that the executives' remuneration is fair and appropriate. Once again, however, it is too easy to assume that there is no need for this role in a business where the executives and the shareholders are the same. Few issues are as divisive in the

owner-managed business as the remuneration of members of
the top team – even though, or perhaps especially, because it's
the boss's decision. A non-exec has a useful role to play as
referee and judge on these issues in even the smallest of businesses. And though the amounts involved may be smaller, a
small business is much more sensitive to the financial pressures brought by executive remuneration than most listed
businesses. The huge remuneration packages of the chief executives of some ailing listed companies may continue to be
woefully inappropriate in spite of the non-execs, but they are
unlikely on their own to bring the business to its knees. This
is not true of many owner-managed, entrepreneurial businesses, the owners of which have been only too willing to
stake the cash health of the business on a bonus for the directors. Conversely, many smaller businesses, particularly family
businesses, under-pay key executives. A conscientious non-
exec can help ensure decisions like this are sensibly thought
through rather than being thinly disguised bets on the future
of the business, or the retention of the executive. A non-exec
can also help ensure that the dividend policy is sensible –
another area where owner-managers have difficulty sorting
out their various interests.

Nomination committee?

Again, in a listed business it is important that processes for
recruiting new directors – particularly a new chief executive –
are objective and transparent, and hence the role of the nomination committee, and of the non-execs who sit on it. In
younger private businesses, a non-exec also has much to add

when the business is planning to build its top team. In particular, she can ensure that the selection process, which is often little more than random, is instead thorough and objective. She can also ensure that the entrepreneur appreciates the need to *complement* the team, rather than just find someone to agree with him – in other words, someone who can help take the team towards the next stage of its evolution.

A related issue of significance is the extent to which the board reviews its own performance. In the owner-managed business, just as in the listed business, the non-exec has a key role to play ensuring individual directors are formally appraised. Non-execs on some boards will find this taxes their powers of persuasion.

Management and strategy

Notwithstanding the previous paragraphs, the non-exec's role

'I look for three key documents when I join the board of a younger business:
1   The accounts, so I can get to grips with the commercial reality, and see if the executives can as well.
2   The strategic plan – there probably isn't one, but creating one will tell the business a lot about where it wants to go and how it's going to get there.
3   An organisation chart – again there probably won't be one of these, but the act of creating one will help sort out job roles, responsibilities and who reports to whom. I usually find that everyone is reporting to the MD – which isn't a good starting point for decent governance or growth.'

in the smaller business is to contribute to management and strategy rather than to corporate governance. As Hampel observes, it is 'particularly in smaller companies [that] non-executive directors may contribute valuable experience not

> **'I get more of a buzz** working as a non-exec in an SME than as one in a PLC – I'm much closer to the coal face.'

otherwise available to management'. In the smaller business it's surely not so much what the non-exec does to the board, or ensures that the board does, as what she brings to the board. The biggest barrier to growth in any growing business is the capability and capacity of the senior management team. A non-exec can help provide valuable experience that may otherwise be in short supply. Besides, the essentials of the business model in the smaller business are likely to be simpler than in a big business, and thus somewhat easier for a part-time non-exec to grasp. The business will sell fewer products, and internal processes are likely to be simpler. A non-exec in a small business will be able to get closer to the day-to-day than in a big business.

Of particular importance are issues relating to growth and the transformation that growth demands. A non-exec, arguing from an independent standpoint, is well placed to counsel the business on the changes that are needed. The greatest of these changes is that to the senior management team itself, its composition and the way it manages itself. Indeed, the roles of the individuals making up the team have to change as the business 'grows up'. The non-exec to the smaller, growing business finds herself playing the role of team coach.

A discussion about the non-exec's contribution to management and strategy raises again the issue of the boundary between executive and non-executive responsibility in the smaller business discussed in the last chapter. This is more a theoretical worry than a practical worry in a well-run business. Although non-execs have to be careful to ensure that everyone knows there's a real distinction between being a non-exec and a part-time exec, clear reporting lines and *de facto* channels of command indicate to staff and others which members of the board really do have operational responsibilities. Clarity on these issues is helped by documentation. Many experienced non-execs see the first 'organisation chart' as an important coming of age for the young business. Non-execs, without direct man-management responsibilities, and appearing on the premises only two or three times a month, are manifestly not in a position to exercise executive control. They are able to test the appropriateness of strategy, but their influence is necessarily exercised through the executives rather than around them. An important issue, therefore, is whether the non-exec has more influence on one member of the board than on another. Even if (inevitably) a non-exec will spend more time with some members of the board than others, she will be most effective in her role if she is available to the board as a whole and to all of its members. This is an independence issue, of course, as was noted in the previous chapter. Being closer to some board members than others can compromise a non-exec's effectiveness and she should work hard to counter this tendency.

A non-executive director doesn't exercise influence just through the directors. Some of the non-executive's most important meetings are not board meetings and they take place outside the boardroom. 'I need my non-execs least in the boardroom,' argues one owner-manager. 'Letting them talk to my senior managers is where they add most value.' Freedom to roam within the business is critically important for an effective non-exec. There is a job to be done building (and repairing) bridges with suppliers, key customers, financiers, industry associations, competitors, regulators and so forth. Indeed, good non-executives are also well connected – in the sense, of course, of being well connected to the people that matter to the business. A non-executive director in the owner-managed business may not be the eyes and ears of the shareholders, but her eyes and ears are important nevertheless. Strategy and management are not just about command and control. They are far more about listening and learning. If you're close to decision-making, there's a huge temptation to listen only to what you want to hear. A key role for a non-executive in an owner-managed business is to hear what needs to be heard, and then convert it, credibly, convincingly and persuasively, into what needs to be said.

Board discipline

For many people, the most significant difference between the attitudes of big, listed businesses and of private, entre-preneurial businesses towards non-execs is symbolised by the fact that in the former the top job is more often than not split between a chief executive and a non-executive chairman,

'A non-exec frequently has a role to play ensuring a fair hearing is given to all important points of view.'

whereas many of the latter are under the control of an all-powerful (and too powerful) entrepreneur. The way boards run in private businesses is therefore different; the distinction between governance and direction less defined.

But here again there are issues for the private, owner-managed business. There are situations in the owner-managed business where a non-executive chair can be hugely advantageous. Family businesses in particular often have much to gain. Perhaps this is unsurprising: in many ways, a family business, sitting as it does on top of sets of sometimes conflicting and sometimes overlapping family issues and business issues, is similar to a big listed company, worried

> **'Dad was chairman,** Mum was also on the board. Son was the commercial director of an entirely different business. Dad wanted Son to take the family business over. Son was reluctant to join the business whilst Dad was still in charge. The business recruited a non-executive chairman acceptable to Dad and Son. Dad turned into a non-exec, Mum stepped down from the board, Son joined the board as an executive to learn the business before taking it over. It's all been a great success. The chairman was key to the transition – in great part because he really understood how values work in a family-owned business.'

about managing its business and its shareholders. Specific instances include the transfer of the business from one family generation to another, and the appointment of 'joint managing directors' as an alternative to appointing one sibling or the other when neither is ready or interested. Even if not formally the chairman, a non-exec frequently has a role to play in the team leading the family business as a 'facilitator' – ensuring a fair hearing is given to all important points of view, and no judgement escapes without a robust challenge. In family businesses the interests of non-family directors and managers often need particular attention from the non-execs, as do the interests of non-working family.

And you should still expect the role to be part-time…!

What a growing business needs from a non-exec:

▪ Ensuring the board discharges its board functions properly – maintaining boardroom discipline, keeping to the agenda, separating shareholder issues from operational issues, etc. – maybe acting as chairman

▪ Objectivity – e.g. when directors' remuneration is discussed, when there's an issue raised by the auditors, and when recruiting a new director

▪ Helping the business develop connections with customers, suppliers, financiers, industry contacts, etc.

▪ First challenge to management information – accounts, internal communications, press releases, business plans, strategy documents, etc.

▪ A sounding board for executives when they are developing or revising strategy

▪ Providing counsel to the board and board members individually

4

Finding and paying a non-executive director

SO YOU'VE DECIDED you want a non-exec – but where do you get one? And how much should you pay? As the role becomes more demanding and less of a sinecure, finding one becomes more problematic and the price rises.

Sometimes you do not have many options. Raising funding from a venture capitalist, for example, often involves the VC asking for a seat on the board. You may expect a choice – but don't expect too much of one.

But even when the search for a non-exec is your idea rather than someone else's, the choice may be limited. The recruitment of all directors – but non-execs in particular – is one area of the economy where the free market seems to let everyone down. If you believe some of those involved in finding non-execs, there is an acute shortage of decent candidates for the role of non-exec in big business. Research shows that 46 of the FTSE 100 companies have to share at least one member of their remuneration committee with another FTSE 100 company, while just 392 directors made up the remuneration committees of 98 of the biggest UK companies[6] – suggesting that the biggest non-exec jobs at least are shared by a relatively small number of individuals. The usual suspects do indeed

'*If you believe some of those involved in finding non-execs, there is an acute shortage of decent candidates.*'

seem to be rather busy. Just fifteen peers and MPs hold more than 150 directorships, according to research by the *Financial Times*.[7] One leading Liberal Democrat holds 21 on his own. It's amazing he has any time for parliamentary business. One could conclude from this concentration of so many directorships in the hands of so few, that there really are only very few who are up to the task. But there are other possible explanations too.

On the hunt – but for what?

In fact there are lots of potential candidates interested in the role. The issue is not so much lack of supply as lack of definition. Increasing the pool of non-execs is a key concern identified by Derek Higgs in his review for the government of the role of non-execs. Indeed, Higgs suggests that the excitement about individuals holding too many directorships has been rather overdone in order to make good copy. He also argues that the pool for potential non-execs is much larger than the one most frequently fished. He is right to argue that the supply could be helped by clarifying the role that non-execs are expected to fulfil, and a greater professionalism in the recruitment process itself. Many boards, in looking for a decent non-exec, are by no means sure what the role consists of. It's hardly surprising therefore that they do not know what sort of individual they are looking for. The easiest thing is for the successful candidate to define the role himself, and the most likely person to be able to define the role in your business is someone who is already fulfilling it in someone else's. No one, as the adage goes, got into trouble for buying from

IBM. Until recently at least, no one got into trouble for recruiting a non-exec who was already a non-exec. As with many easy things, this is lazy thinking.

The lack of confidence in non-exec recruitment processes that afflicts big listed businesses, and which is founded essentially on ignorance, also afflicts private businesses. Indeed, the lack of confidence is even more marked in the private business. My experience suggests that owner-managed businesses are reluctant to turn to a register of non-execs or even to a specialist recruitment agency when looking for a new non-exec, preferring instead to put their trust in family or friends.

There can be a cosy, self-fulfilling cycle here, for family businesses in particular. You want to keep the business in the family – and you are keen therefore to keep the family in the business, even if some parts of the family are reluctant. A non-exec role might be one way of generating a bit of enthusiasm

> **Research conducted** by accountants BDO Stoy Hayward in winter 2002 suggests that of all external advisers, owner-managers prefer to go to their accountants. Indeed, 31 per cent indicated their accountant as their preferred source of advice – compared to 24 per cent who preferred to call a friend. Only 5 per cent indicated their lawyer, and 2 per cent their bank manager.

in an otherwise unenthusiastic family member, but is hardly the best reason for appointing a non-exec, nor the best way of finding the right one for the business.

Registers and agencies should not be discounted but many

of the more forward-thinking owner-managed businesses are most likely to turn to trusted professional sources for advice on potential non-execs. The accountant is a particularly popular port of call – more so nowadays than the bank manager, who is becoming a creature of myth for an increasing number of smaller businesses in particular. Sources such as this are likely to have access to potential non-execs, as well as personal experience of them in action.

Given that most private businesses are unlikely to be impressed by (or interested in) having an MP as non-exec, what sort of individual should they be looking for?

Non-exec positions have often been filled by retired business people, or retired accountants and lawyers. To a certain extent this tendency is driven by supply. In the good old days the title indicated a sinecure rather than an active role. And now that the title does have a serious role and responsibilities to go with it, many are arguing that the job is too dangerous to be done by anyone other than the foolish. Whichever way you look at it, taking on the role of non-exec is hardly a good career move. It is usually part-time, and for a defined period of time – neither of which is likely to make the job more appealing to those facing the demands of bringing up a young family or dealing with a mortgage. Your non-exec – and everyone else's – will have to have a significant income from somewhere else, and have relatively low expectations for future career development. Retirees are less likely to have these worries – and also have the advantage of having experience in abundance – and it's experience that is one of the most important things small businesses are looking for.

For many, however, a retired individual as non-exec sums

up all that is wrong with current thinking about board governance. Someone who is active as an executive elsewhere is far better qualified to act as a non-exec than a retiree, who may seem really only to be after something that keeps him from spending too much time with the wife and that supplements a pension – and certainly not the real challenges that non-execs have to deal with. So it is no surprise that in recent years there has been a shift from retirees to active executives as the best people to be non-executives. Indeed, one of Higgs's less publicised recommendations is an 'invitation' to the chairmen of listed companies 'to encourage and facilitate their executive directors and suitable senior management just below board level to take one non-executive director position on a non-competitor board'.

This sort of thinking is not without its flaws. For starters, 'retired' doesn't mean 'past it'. In the owner-managed sector in particular, there are capable individuals who, as a consequence of selling out, are looking for roles with meaning and challenge but without the commitment that goes with being an executive. In addition, executives active in small business management haven't got the time for paying attention to a non-executive role elsewhere, and I'm a little surprised that Higgs thinks that executives in listed companies have such time. Besides, many of the qualities that you might look for in an executive, you might think twice about in a non-executive. In an interesting article, seasoned non-executive Hamish Guthrie compares a typical advert for an executive with the response by the Institute of Chartered Accountants of England and Wales to Derek Higgs's call for consultation on the role of the non-exec.[8] A typical ad for an executive might read as follows: 'Action-orientated, strong focus on revenue and profit growth, motivational leader able to stretch the boundaries, team player to drive change and deliver against challenging strategy and targets…' On the other hand, Guthrie quotes from the ICAEW response to the Higgs review: 'Independent of mind, with honesty and integrity, curiosity and willingness to challenge results even when they

> **'Some CEOs make lousy non-execs.** They find it impossible not to try and take over – rather than to help the actual executives to cover all the important bases.'

appear to be successful, willing to stand up to executive directors and, if appropriate, resign.' There is indeed a fundamental mismatch here, but not really one between 'retired' and 'active' – more one between the sorts of individuals that are needed on successful boards and how they fit together.

Nonetheless, there are executives who would work well as non-execs – and Higgs's recommendations may foster interest in the area to the particular advantage of smaller businesses. On the face of it, there's a lot that's attractive in this idea. Senior managers in big businesses are often tempted by the prospect of a directorship somewhere else. Indeed, such experience may better prepare them for future roles in their current businesses. On the other hand, smaller businesses often look to their non-execs for help building the controls and management infrastructure needed for the bigger business they hope to become. Additionally, notwithstanding my earlier reservations, a big business is more likely than a small business to be able to flex the workload of its senior management and make the prospect of someone taking on a non-executive directorship sensible. Whether the idea becomes a reality or not remains to be seen. Certainly, for all the good reasons in favour of the idea, there are plenty of problems – not least conflicts of time and interest.

It is important when recruiting a non-exec that you carefully define the qualities you are looking for – and that you expect, indeed demand, that they are different from those you see in your executives. As with all new board appointments to a growing, entrepreneurial business, a new non-exec has to add to the board rather than merely reinforce it. The following list might do for starters:

- Broad business experience – including, but not restricted to your sector or your size of business
- The ability to assess people and situations analytically and dispassionately
- The ability to hold one's ground – but also the ability to persuade others of the validity of one's own point of view
- Financial literacy and experience – able to read, write, understand and speak the languages of corporate finance and management accounting
- Awareness of the legal environment and the duties and obligations owed to other parties and stakeholders, both by the directors and the company
- Familiarity with best board practice, and how this might be interpreted for a business the size of yours
- The ability to act as a sounding board for other directors –

which implies approachability as well as first-class
interpersonal and communication skills, in particular an
ability to listen and understand
- A sense of humour
- A sense of humility – particularly if they are experienced
executives in their own right

The personal skills listed here are even more important
than the technical ones, and are certainly more difficult to
look for in a recruitment process. Derek Higgs sums up these
personal qualities excellently in his report: 'Non-executive
directors need to be sound in judgement and to have an
inquiring mind. They should question intelligently, debate
constructively, challenge rigorously and decide dispassionately. And they should listen sensitively.' His words apply as
much to private business non-execs as to listed business non-
execs.

Good process

Businesses need to ensure that their process for selecting a
non-exec is at the least as robust and impartial as that used
for selecting their executive directors. In addition to the
usual checks on CVs and references, it is important to ensure
personal chemistry is right. Either in formal interview or
informal meeting the candidate will need to meet all the
important people in the business – for his benefit as well as
for that of the business. Meetings between candidates and
outside advisers (auditors in particular) can be mutually beneficial. It should never be forgotten that in all recruitment

processes, but particularly those involving the most important positions, two selections are going on: the business is selecting the individual, but the individual is also selecting the business.

Impartiality is critical – even the smallest details in a process can cause it to backfire. One family business was looking to recruit a non-exec to represent the interests of non-working family members. The board short-listed candidates. Each candidate was invited to an informal chat with family members over a pint of beer at the local. But one candidate was unable to make his meeting. When the meeting was rescheduled for a gathering at the chairman's house, some family members immediately assumed that the candidate was the chairman's 'favourite' and refused to take him seriously as a candidate.

A process can be helped by using recruitment professionals, of course. But you don't need recruitment professionals to guarantee the discipline and structure that characterise a good process. However, outside advisers are most useful in helping you get the brief right in the first place. Your process should start with a clear, agreed and documented statement as to what you are looking for, followed by agreed, documented mechanisms for ensuring the candidates have those qualities. And your process should be applied scrupulously to all short-listed candidates. Each candidate should have the same structured interviews and the same informal meetings. If one candidate sits a test the others should sit the same one. And all evidence should be collected and documented – including in particular the subjective assessments formed of personality. Lastly, you should believe the evidence you collect. Too many selection processes break down at the last hurdle when 'gut feel' is given higher priority than hard evidence.

Even the best process can deliver a wrong candidate. It is imperative that the new non-exec and the company should be able to walk away from the deal in the first six months without penalty.

What's in the package?

How to pay a non-exec is a hugely controversial topic, tied up as it is with all the key issues of competence, commitment, value and independence. Pay a non-exec too much, or promise him a fortune some time in the future dependent on this or that, and his independence will be compromised: a non-exec who cannot walk away will never be entirely independent. For most non-execs, however, the opposite problem is true. Pay a non-exec too little and you're less likely to find someone who will add value.

A survey conducted for ITNEA,[9] an organisation representing non-execs to the IT industry, suggests that the average non-exec chairman is paid £44,520 for 47 days a year, and the average standard non-executive director gets £16,974 for 21 days a year – not much over £800 a day. Put another way, this compares favourably with the time cost of a junior management consultant. Non-execs don't and can't do it only for the money – they're in it for more than that. But the corollary of this is that a non-executive who adds good value may still turn out to be surprisingly cheap – certainly compared to the cost of an executive or an adviser.

However, as the demands placed on non-execs increase, so

does the pressure on remuneration. Businesses are inevitably exploring other forms of remuneration – bonuses, shares or share options are becoming increasingly common. The Top Pay Research Group reported in 2001 that the proportion of non-execs who hold options in the companies they serve had increased from 3 per cent to 18 per cent since 1998. If the US experience is anything to go by then we have much further to go. According to Korn/Ferry, in the US some 75 per cent of outside directors have options in the companies they direct.[10]

Giving directors options, or even equity, has often been the route to making them very rich if they happen to work for major listed companies. In smaller businesses it's more likely to be an excuse for not paying them properly in the first place. In any case, there are independence concerns about equity-based remuneration for non-execs. On the one hand, if a non-exec is rewarded in effect for increasing shareholder value, then surely she is being motivated to add value and safeguard the interests of the shareholders. The ITNEA research referred to above notes that 'the majority of non-executives in the IT sector feel that such rewards [share options] should be part of the package and that they do align interests with share-holders'. On the other hand, the National Association of Pension Funds comes out against non-execs having options, arguing that the 'greater leverage' involved could compromise decision making.[11] One of the key roles of non-execs is to establish the parameters for rewarding executives – many of whom will also have equity-based remuneration. Equity-based remuneration for the non-execs might encourage them to be too close to the execs.

Yet it is a fact that one of the commonest conditions

imposed on any young business by a financier is the require-
ment to have a seat on the board. Equity holding and non-
executive status go hand in hand it seems.

Higgs concludes that there is 'some merit' in giving non-
executive directors the opportunity to take part of their remuneration in the form of shares in lieu of cash. But he concludes
that they should not hold options, arguing that options are
more likely to encourage holders to pay undue attention to
share price rather than to underlying performance. If options
are used, Higgs recommends that shareholder approval is
sought in advance, and that the non-exec should be required
to keep any shares acquired via the option for at least a year
after leaving the board.

It should not be forgotten, of course, that options and
equity in a private business are very different matters to
options and equity in a listed business. Equity in a listed business is much more liquid. Equity or an option over equity in
a private business is only worth something if the director gets
the chance to convert it into cash – which may well have the
effect of focusing a director's attention on a future trade sale
or other form of owner-exit. Again, such an arrangement is
hardly conducive to fostering independence. If you are deter-
mined to use equity-based remuneration, the best advice is to
structure a no-cost or penalty exit for both parties in the first
six months as part of the agreement, thus ensuring that both
parties are not bound by a long-term, costly manacle before
they are sure they like each other.

There are other aspects of the package to consider. Most
seem agreed about bonuses and other short-term, profit-
related incentives, however. Non-execs in even the smallest

businesses have a key role in determining the bonuses of others. This should be the closest they get to a bonus themselves. And the same goes for most other aspects of a 'typical' remuneration package. At the heart of the issue is the fact that non-execs don't, and should not, see themselves as employees, and are consequently not entitled to the benefits that go with employment in the first place. A non-exec gets fees, not a salary. Nor should he expect a hefty termination package. Ian Hay Davison, in his 'Open Letter to a New Non-executive Director', suggests that non-execs should expect either six or twelve months' notice as part of the deal – but that they should expect to work it out, and not to get it in the form of a golden handshake.[12] The contrasting recent experience of many executives is worth noting.

Perhaps the best benefit any non-exec could get – and one all too often forgotten – is Directors' and Officers' Insurance, thus offering some peace of mind if the company gets into trouble and shareholders start looking for someone to blame. Indeed, 'D&O' should be part of the standard terms of any director, non-executive or executive. The insurance premiums should be tax deductible for the company if the company pays them – or tax deductible for the individual, should the latter have to foot the bill herself. The insurance does not guarantee complete peace of mind. In the current litigious environment, insurance can be increasingly expensive and difficult to get, particularly for business interests in the USA. Insurance policies may also come with onerous terms or caps. In addition, directors need to be careful to distinguish insurance designed to protect directors and officers from insurance designed to protect professional advisers. The second category is covered

'The role of non-exec, even in a small business, is nothing if not increasingly risky.'

by professional indemnity insurance. Some individuals advising smaller businesses need to be sure of which category they fall into, and that all necessary risks are covered. Nevertheless, Directors' and Officers' Insurance should be taken very seriously, by the company as well as by the individual director.

There are, as always, tax issues to worry about – but a discussion of some of the most important of these is relegated to the 'Useful information' chapter at the end. However, before closing this chapter it is important to stress that the relationship between a non-executive and his company should be documented. The document is unlikely to be an employment contract, but it will state the duties the non-exec is expected to discharge, in return for what package. Documentation should also be drafted that defines the relationship between the non-exec and the executive and the board – defining and circumscribing the respective duties of each to their business and to each other, as well as defining the types of decisions that need to be referred to whom. Again, a key issue here is distinguishing between a non-exec's activities as director, and his activities as an adviser – and how he gets paid for each. As with all spheres of business life, the more duties can be defined and documented, the more business risks can be managed – particularly given that the role of non-executive continues to be hazily defined in law. And the role of non-exec, even in a small business, is nothing if not increasingly risky.

- The fact that so many big companies seem to share non-execs doesn't mean they are impossible to find
- Your accountant is probably a good source of leads for a new non-exec
- Ex-executives don't necessarily make good non-executives
- You want your non-execs to have different qualities and experience from your execs
- Non-execs are cheap – compared at least to executives and advisers
- Equity-based remuneration is increasingly popular – but beware of the dangers of compromising a non-exec's independence

5

Growth and the non-executive director

THE FACT IS THAT NON-EXECS are relatively rare in small businesses. Research conducted by BDO Stoy Hayward for the *Sunday Times* Enterprise Network in the winter of 2002 indicated that 28 per cent of their members had a non-executive director. Research conducted for the Association of Chartered Certified Accountants suggests that only a minority of SMEs have a non-exec – indeed, in businesses with fewer than 50 employees, fewer than 20 per cent of companies bother. For businesses with between 200 and 400 employees, the proportion with non-execs rises to almost a half. Their data suggests a slightly more complex picture: businesses are more likely to have non-execs in their *very* earliest stages than they are shortly afterwards – maybe suggesting that at formation businesses use non-execs to borrow credibility. But, it would appear to be at 50 employees that SMEs get 'more likely' to engage a non-exec.

In reality, the need for a non-exec is more an attitude of mind to management and direction than a function of size. Certainly, when the business's founders find themselves evolving into a board and start thinking of themselves as such, this is the time when they will first derive significant benefit from non-execs. The evolution of the top team is critical for any growing business – indeed, there's a lot of evidence to suggest that the capability and capacity of the top management team is the biggest constraint on growth. Not only will an ambitious management team realise this – it will realise that the outside world of potential clients and financiers will realise it too. Decent non-execs not only add to a team's capability: they will also ensure that more is made of the skills and capabilities of the other team members. They also add to a team's credibility. A team eager for growth will recruit a non-exec before the City demands that they have one.

Part of the challenge faced by the board of the growing business is change. Fast-growing, entrepreneurial businesses

> **'I joined one design and animation business** as non-exec. The business was still small, but was profitable and growing fast. We worked hard at raising finance without risking the founder losing control. But the founder eventually decided that he didn't want the pressures that went with running a business. The business has now closed, and he's gone back to being self-employed. Growth is about whether the founders have got the bottle for it. All a non-exec can do is help.'

can flip from success to failure very quickly – and the margin for error is very small, even in a business earning big margins. Businesses also change as they grow, and the faster they grow, the faster they change.

For the inexperienced, the real problem might seem to be the pace of growth. If the change that growth brings worries

'The issue is not so much the pace of growth as how that growth is supported and sustained.'

you, it is easy to conclude that you should try to slow down growth. But being able to build a business that is sustainable before the competition can get at you often dictates the necessity for swift growth, particularly in the early stages. Slowing growth to a rate that is comfortable is a big business response to a small business problem. The issue is not so much the pace of growth as how that growth is supported and sustained, and it is here that an experienced non-exec can help significantly.

One of the best descriptions of the sort of organisational problems created inside entrepreneurial businesses is Robert Simons's 'Risk Exposure Calculator'.[13] Convert the questions in the framework into numbers and you can develop some sort of picture of the organisational risk inherent in your company, and also some idea of the priority areas for the attention of the non-executive.

Growth	Pressure for performance		Rate of expansion		Inexperience of employees	
	?	+	?	+	?	=
Culture	Rewards for entrepreneurial risk taking		Executive resistance to bad news		Level of internal competition	
	?	+	?	+	?	=
Information management	Transaction complexity and velocity		Gaps in diagnostic performance measures		Degree of decentralised decision making	
	?	+	?	+	?	=

Reading across the top line, growth brings its own problems – particularly if exacerbated by pressures to perform (from a venture capitalist, for example). The second line, culture, draws attention to key entrepreneurial characteristics that are easier to manage in a small organisation when everyone knows everyone, but are less manageable when the organisation gets bigger, and when its well-being can be threatened if internal competition gets out of control. The bottom line draws attention to control and measurement mechanisms, the extent to which they capture all aspects of business performance and the extent to which they evolve as the business grows. The framework is hardly scientific, but there's lots here to give a non-exec food for thought.

The role of the non-exec also has to evolve, of course, as the business evolves. Young businesses, and those run by young people in particular, can be forgiven for having to find their way around law and regulation. Smaller businesses value financial expertise in their non-execs as well. Most business managers are reluctant to confess to inadequacies in their abilities to read and interpret financial information. Younger, inexperienced directors are more reluctant than most, no matter how successful they are. In fact, the more successful, the more reluctant. It is down to the non-exec to see to it that the directors really can read the dials – or at least understand the story. Many communication failings at the top of businesses can be traced to the unwillingness of someone, somewhere to ask questions and seek clarification. The non-exec has much to add to the financial management of a young business, but she also has much to add merely by being fearless about asking questions that are too dumb for anyone else to have the guts to ask.

There are other changes as the business grows. In the smaller business the non-exec will be towards the 'executive' end of the scale – or rather more conscious of the need to plug

> **'One family-owned business** was looking for £10 million or so from a trade sale. Advisers were in place, and the deal was being fronted by a non-exec chairman. The chairman unfortunately died. A new chair was appointed, who rapidly concluded that, though the old chair had done a great job in guiding the business through its early stages, he had no experience of a trade sale at all – and far too much reliance was being placed on the advisers. It was the new chairman who advised a nervous family to turn down a £15 million offer. The business eventually went for £18 million.'

the gaps in the executive team – than in the big business. As the business grows the role shifts from plugging gaps to focusing on ensuring that the executive members of the team cover all the bases themselves, effectively and efficiently – that the whole is greater than the sum of its parts. This is facilitation rather than execution.

As the business gets bigger, the non-exec should find herself developing more channels of communication and influence, outside as well as inside the boardroom. Meetings with middle management, for example, will become increasingly important. The bigger the organisation, the less 'complete' will be the information passed along official networks. As always, it is the story that people don't want to tell that is just as important as the story they do want to tell. Surprise visits to factories or showrooms can be more useful, to both

'It is the story that people don't want to tell that is just as important as the story they do want to tell.'

the factory and the non-exec, than presentations in the board-room.

A bigger business will look to get more from its non-exec in terms of corporate governance. Governance roles will be formalised as membership of the audit, remuneration and appointment committees. But there are other aspects of big business management that are particularly important, although they are of less importance in the smaller business,

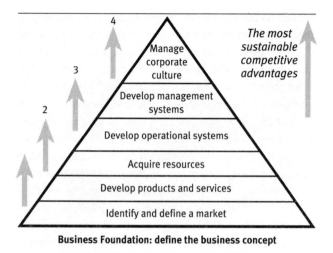

Business Foundation: define the business concept

and to which a non-exec can make a significant contribution.

The above illustration is based on the work of Eric Flamholtz and Yvonne Randle.[14] It's one of many diagrammatic representations of what happens to businesses as they grow. These representations are sometimes called 'growth models'. What's particularly interesting is the distinction they draw between growing a business and building a *sustainable* business. The role that the development of corporate culture and management systems play in this is crucial. Management systems will come as no surprise to anyone – the bigger business needs a management infrastructure to survive. And if it is the role of the executives to run the infrastructure, the non-executives have a key role in building it. Perhaps more subtle is the importance of organisational culture. Small businesses are run on personality, and the personality is usually that of the founder. But this isn't sufficient for the bigger business, in which the personal influence of the entrepreneur is inevitably diluted the further it has to reach. Culture, an artificial construct, is what is needed to fill the void internally – an amalgam of mission, business plan, building layout, values and human resources policy. Luck need have little to do with it – unless you let it. In place of the *external* influence of the entrepreneur, of course, you have brand management. All of these things can be constructed dispassionately – and managers who are too close to the business can find it very difficult to identify and define the elements in what they do instinctively that will need distilling into culture. A big business will call on consultants to help with this sort of thing – but in the first instance a non-exec can help far more cost-effectively and with a far more immediate impact. But make no mistake, the transitions outlined here are significant and have huge implications for the senior management team. Even those who can appreciate the significance of the change in theory may have problems delivering it in practice.

The way in which the non-exec role changes as the business grows and develops begs some important questions about non-exec development and education. On the one hand, as the next chapter makes clear, being a non-exec is not a career. Just as it is unlikely that the founder will grow and evolve with his business as it passes through all its stages of development and the changes that go with them, so it is unlikely that a non-exec will follow suit. For the non-exec in the entrepreneurial business, just as for the entrepreneur, it is a question of when, not whether, to leave.

On the other hand, a non-exec needs to make the most of his changing times in a growing business, and non-exec skills development is an important issue – but not one that is well served. According to a survey sponsored by KPMG and reported in November 2002, more than half of non-execs have never had a formal appraisal of their work, and most admit lacking adequate training. Notwithstanding the increase in pressures foisted on to non-execs, the role continues to be one of the last bastions of gentlemanly amateurism. Good non-execs are seemingly born, not made. There are few forums for exploring and promoting the particular concerns of the non-exec – and those that exist are relatively new and untried. Higgs writes that 'There should be a step change in training and development provision so that it is suited to the needs of boards.' The problem is even more acute for non-execs in smaller, entrepreneurial businesses. If most business development is aimed at the executive rather than the non-executive, it is also aimed at the big business rather than the small business. Even though a non-exec is unlikely to stay with the business from foundation to full listing, he will cer-

> **'A £10 million services business** hit hard times. Rather than make good use of the considerable skills and experience of the non-execs on the board whom he had worked hard to recruit, the founder "reverted to type" and attempted to take hands-on control of all aspects of the business.'

tainly see it through several major transformations as it grows. Being able to assist the business not only where it is

'For the non-exec in the entrepreneurial business, just as for the entrepreneur, it is a question of when, not whether, to leave.'

now, but also where it needs to get to (as well as having some understanding of where it comes from) demands a breadth of experience and expertise that is hard to come by.

Non-execs learn most from non-execs. Forums that offer opportunities for non-execs to meet and exchange ideas

---

- Non-execs are still fairly rare in smaller businesses – more's the pity
- Growth means change – including changes for the role of the non-exec
- Control systems in particular come under pressure as the business expands
- The contribution of the non-exec needs to be kept under continual review. As with all senior staff, non-execs need appraising and training
- Non-execs need to know when to leave

enable them to share experiences and approaches to problems. Again, it is accountants and bankers who are most likely to provide occasions for this kind of exchange with their technical updates and networking sessions. Who you meet will in all likelihood be more interesting than what you hear from the platform. As far as technical education and support is concerned, an increasing amount is provided on the internet, and some sources are provided at the end of the book.

6

Endgames and new games

Walking away

The ability to walk away is one of the defining characteristics
of a non-executive – or at least it should be. A meaningful
threat of resignation is the best demonstration of independence from the company. Resigning is difficult if you depend
too much on the income you derive from the company. It is
also difficult if you are too attached to any part of the
company, or if you are tied up in current business that should
more properly have been left to the executives. Again, it is also
more difficult if you've been involved with the business for a
long time. Lastly, of course, resigning is difficult if you have
been placed as a non-exec to represent the interests of a particular stakeholder – a venture capitalist, for example.

If the ability to resign is a defining characteristic,
knowing the right moment to resign is one of the best tests
of judgement for a non-executive. For most non-executives,
though, resignation should be a matter of course. Commenting on the spectacular fall in Cable & Wireless's share
price in the autumn of 2002, the newspapers were quick to
point out that at least one of their non-executives had been

'Knowing the right moment to resign is one of the best tests of judgement for a non-executive.'

in office since the late 1980s. With due respect to the individual concerned, longevity is not necessarily a sign of success. If your job is to give an independent view, then there can be an advantage to being fresh. And careful readers will remember our quoting at the start of this book Lord Young's view that the role of non-exec should be done away with altogether – and they will remember also that he is an ex-chairman of Cable & Wireless. Maybe there's a connection here – or maybe not. At any rate, the principle holds good for owner-managed businesses as much as for listed ones. When signing up a non-executive, wherever possible you should have the endgame in mind. One entrepreneur argues that it's a good idea to agree the terms of the resignation letter when the non-exec is recruited. To start with, either party should be able to terminate the arrangement for whatever reason and without financial penalty within the first six months. A non-executive relationship, like any other, may just not work, and this may not become evident until you try it.

Thereafter a non-exec should recognise that he adds most value to a company by being associated with it for the right period of time. Too short an association, and the learning curve is too steep. Too long an association, and, with the best will in the world, the non-exec will become too involved, too close and too partial. The best arrangement for most is for the appointment to be terminable after no more than three years. On the assumption that the skills brought to the business by the non-exec are still valid – and they might well not be in the rapidly changing world of the growing business –

'**A family business recruited a new MD** to groom a business for listing on the USM. The overall strategy involved recruiting an experienced non-exec, developing internal controls and systems, and persuading the family board members to step down from key executive positions. Everyone agreed with the approach – but in the end the family couldn't step down. The MD and the non-exec resigned.'

---

renewing the arrangement for a second three-year term could be beneficial. At the end of the second term, however, both the director and the company should think very carefully before renewing the arrangement – even if the director is still perceived as having relevant skills. Certainly the particular reasons for his appointment are likely to have long ago become irrelevant by the time it is appropriate for him to leave – especially if the business is successful. This is most likely to happen if part of his role is to supervise the development of the executive team, and compensate for its shortcomings in the meantime. If he does his job properly, many a non-exec will find he has made himself redundant. A possible exception to this generalisation might be if the director in question is going to spend some time as non-executive chairman.

The approach outlined above may sound puritanical. But if you're not serious about it, then you're probably not serious about the real role of a non-executive director. As a non-exec you trade day-to-day contact for independence of mind. A non-exec is there to give fresh thinking, and to challenge the views of the executives. And once the non-exec has worked his way up to the top of the learning curve, fresh thinking becomes more and more difficult the longer the relationship progresses.

A director may of course wish to resign before the expiry of his term of office. During 2002 it became only too evident when non-execs should have resigned from big, listed businesses: when executives have refused to accept the collective accountability of the board, for instance; when the non-execs have disagreed fundamentally on matters of strategy; or when non-execs have detected or merely suspected that information has been withheld or the interests of shareholders and other important stakeholders not safeguarded. I am sure there are non-executive directors of Enron and Worldcom who went down with the ship, but who now wish they had shouted a little louder when they first saw the iceberg – or even when

'Non-executives have to be increasingly sensitive to their place in the firing line if things go wrong.'

the captain first told them of plans to steer into icy waters. But these are all big-ticket, high-profile, big business examples. Is there anything different about the role of the non-exec in the smaller business?

Yes and no, of course. A non-exec in an owner-managed business is far more likely to be instrumental in ensuring that the right information is generated in the first place than he is to be struggling to understand the information generated by the executives. But non-executives have to be increasingly sensitive, even in small businesses, to their place in the firing line if things go wrong. They might come across fraud or bribery or other forms of wrongdoing – small businesses aren't exempt from this sort of thing just because they may be owner-managed. Stakeholders will look for ways of recovering their losses, and the non-executive – particularly if wealthy – may seem an attractive target, whether or not he is insured. A non-exec in a small business is just as much advised to ensure he is heard and has influence as in a big business, and should take just as seriously the threat of the ultimate sanction. Resigning mid-term is always an action of last resort, of course – but it is still an important weapon in the non-exec's armoury.

New agendas

The role of non-exec is under increasing scrutiny. In response to accounting and governance scandals, governments have been swift to commission reviews and investigations. Not all of these have been fully thought through, and as always there is a danger that the smaller firm may get caught in the cross-fire. The introduction in 2002 of the so-called Sarbanes-Oxley Act in the USA is an indication of how far legalisation could develop, with its panoply of draconian prison sentences and its imposition of oaths on financial officers and chief executives. Although Sarbanes-Oxley only affects companies listed in the States, it indicates the level of legalisation that may soon affect companies elsewhere. And it may be only a matter of time before non-execs in listed companies are under pressure to formalise their responsibility for preventing accounting scandals. Changes to non-execs in listed businesses will inevitably influence non-execs in smaller businesses.

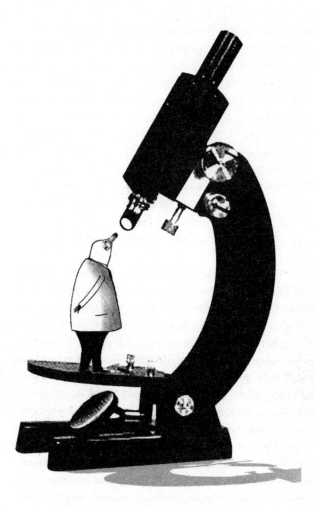

'The role of non-exec is under increasing scrutiny.'

In my view, legislators and rule makers should think very carefully before taking action. In the UK, the Higgs report, published in January 2003, is far more considered in its conclusions and its recommendations than the Sarbanes-Oxley legislation in the US. Higgs likens the hastily passed legislation in the US to the legislation in the UK enacted to deal with dangerous dogs. He rightly shies away from legislation, recommending instead the code-based approach established by Hampel and Cadbury. The code approach 'offers flexibility and intelligent discretion and allows for the valid exception to the sound rule. The brittleness and rigidity of legislation cannot dictate the behaviour or foster the trust, [that] I believe is fundamental to . . . superior corporate performance.'

But, as noted throughout this book, Higgs – for all the strengths of his review – is really dealing with the big, listed business. There is a lot in the Higgs report that should be of interest to owner-managed businesses, and I recommend that anyone interested in the recruiting a non-exec in a private business, or interested in becoming a non-exec to one, should read it. It also benefits from being exceptionally well written and thus easy and interesting to read. But, for all the good things about the Higgs report, sorting out the role of non-exec in the smaller business isn't simply a matter of scaling down Higgs.

Indeed, right at the heart of the issue is a fundamentally different problem. The huge majority of listed companies have non-execs – most have several. Most private businesses, on the other hand, don't have a non-exec. They don't appreciate what it is that a non-executive can add to the capability of the team, the quality and robustness of its decision-taking, the strength of its connections with the outside world. They don't appreciate how a good non-executive can add a safeguard against the risks of entrepreneurship. They also just don't appreciate what *good value* a non-exec can be.

If, in closing, I suggest that those entrepreneurial businesses who've had the same non-execs for too long should think about changing them, so I also suggest that those businesses who reckon they have managed perfectly well so far without a non-exec consider changing their minds. Despite the lack of legal obligation, or of well-publicised sets of guidelines and recommendations, my contention is that the well-managed and well-advised ambitious, owner-managed business of the future will be foolish to be without one.

7

Useful information

Non-executive directors' remuneration – some tax issues

A director, whether executive or non-executive, is an officer of the company and no distinction is made between the two in the Taxes Acts. Income in respect of an office is chargeable to tax under Schedule E and S131 TA 1988.

Inland Revenue concessions

There is a published Inland Revenue extra-statutory concession that allows the director's fees to be paid without deducting tax in certain circumstances:

1 Where the fees are received by a member of a professional practice, or
2 Where the director is required to pass the fees to a limited company and does so.

These two concessions will only be given where certain other conditions are met, so it's important to take advice.

In general, however, PAYE should be deducted when paying fees to a director personally – including a non-exec director. A company should treat the director as though he was a normal employee and submit a completed form P46 to the Inland Revenue so that the correct number can be obtained and operated.

There are special rules for accounting for National Insurance contributions on directors' remuneration. It may be possible for the director to obtain deferment of the employee's Class 1 NIC, but this will depend on his personal circumstances.

It is perfectly possible for a director to provide services to a company in a separate capacity. For instance, he could invoice the company for services provided as a consultant under Schedule D if he had specialist knowledge. It is possible to imagine an individual receiving both Schedule D and Schedule E income. There would be no such scope for this, however, if the fees were being paid merely for duties as a director, such as attendance at board meetings, etc.

Where a director's fees have been paid gross in the past, a switch should be made. The Inland Revenue rarely view this as serious, but will review his personal tax affairs to ensure the fees have been declared on his tax returns and subjected to tax.

However, the payment of National Insurance contributions can be more of a problem when you switch to PAYE status. Where an employee's NICs are due, the Revenue may be prepared to calculate what is due under Class 1 and deduct from that the total of Class 2 and Class 4 NICs that have been paid on a self-employed basis. It's important to note that an employee's NICs become the liability of the employer in such cases. The normal employer's NIC also remains due and payable and it is possible for the Inland Revenue to charge penalties as well as interest.

As an attempt to get around the problem, some directors have set up their own personal service companies. Provided the basic paperwork is in order, payment could be made to that company on the production of an invoice. However, the Inland Revenue have got wise to this, and the introduction of IR35 has generated some notoriety as an attempt to plug what some see as a loophole. The IR35 legislation applies only to an individual who would have been an employee were it not for the insertion of a limited service company between him and the 'employer'. A non-executive director is an office-holder, and if the only relationship with the third party is as a non-executive director, then the rules will not apply.

The legislation may bite, however, if there are other services performed for the client through the service company. In these circumstances the individual may be both an office-holder and an employee. A non-executive director will be caught by the National Insurance regulations. This is because these regulations will apply where an individual would have been an 'employed earner' without the insertion of the service company. The term 'employed earner' includes an office-holder.

Other reading

The Guide for Non-executive Directors, jointly published by Hanson Green and Ashurst Morris Crisp, 2000. An easy-to-read guide to the duties of the non-exec.

The Role of Non-executive Director in United Kingdom SMEs
by Berry & Perren, and published by the Certified
Accountants Educational Trust, 2000. A piece of
academic research, but an interesting and readable survey
of current practice and attitudes.

The Independent Director: The role and contribution of non-executive directors, Kogan Page, 1999. Contains some
useful information.

The BDO Guide to the Family Business, Peter Leach and Tony
Bogod, Kogan Page, 1999. A treasure trove of insights
for those involved in family businesses.

www.independentdirector.co.uk A useful site providing
information, news releases, briefings, etc. for non-execs.
Mostly aimed at big businesses, but still some things here
for everyone.

If recruiting a non-exec, or hoping to be recruited as one, try:
www.exec-appointments.com
www.nonexecdirector.co.uk
www.nedexchange.co.uk
These sites may point you in the right direction if you're
looking for a non-exec. And they also provide some useful
ancillary information.

~ Boyden

. IOD non executive register.

. uccs

8

Acknowledgements

THE TEXT OF THIS BOOK has benefited from discussions with many of my partners at BDO Stoy Hayward. But I single out Simon Bevan and Peter Leach in particular. Perhaps even more significant have been discussions with people who have held the role. There are too many of these to name them all individually, but I mention in particular David Treadwell, Oliver Stanley, and Colin Barrow. For the tax note in Chapter 7, I thank in particular Frank Goldberg at BDO Stoy Hayward. Drafts of the text have also been read by Tony Bogod, Philip Rubenstein, and Charles Boundy of Fladgate Fielder, to whom many thanks.

Thanks lastly to those at home. These things inevitably are written mostly at home when you should be concentrating on other matters.

9

Notes

1 *Financial Times*, April 2002
2 *Review of the Role and Effectiveness of Non-executive Directors*, Derek Higgs (HMSO, January 2003)
3 *The Role of Non-executive Directors in United Kingdom SMEs*, Berry and Perren (Certified Accountants Educational Trust, 2000)
4 As reported by Arthur Levitt, former chairman of the SEC, in the *Financial Times*, November 2002
5 *Independent Director* newsletter No. 8, Winter 2001/2002
6 Labour Research, July 1999
7 *Financial Times*, August 2002
8 'Can leopards change their spots?', *Accountancy*, December 2002
9 ITNEA in association with Inbucon, July 1999
10 Reported in *Financial Times*, October 2001
11 *Financial Times*, May 2002
12 In *Boardroom Governance Practical Insights* (ICAEW, 1999)
13 In *Performance Measurement and Control Systems*, Robert Simons (2000)
14 *Growing Pains: Transitioning from an Entrepreneurship to a*

Professionally Managed Firm, Eric Flamholtz & Yvonne Randle (Jossey-Bass, 2000)

Current and forthcoming BDO titles

Finance Directors
A BDO Stoy Hayward Guide for Growing Businesses
by Rupert Merson

What is the role of the finance director in a smaller or medium-sized business with ambitions to grow? And what is the experience of working as a finance director in an entrepreneurial environment actually like?

Rupert Merson's entertaining, informative and up-to-date guide is intended for both the entrepreneur and the potential finance director. Straightforward and practical, it is the essential introduction to the subject.

ISBN 1 86197 454 X

£6.99

Managing Directors
A BDO Stoy Hayward Guide for Growing Businesses
by Rupert Merson

Part inventor, part entrepreneur, part manager, part accountant, part leader, part salesman, part bottle-washer – the role
of managing director in the younger, growing business is one
of the most demanding jobs in commerce today. Yet it is surprisingly little written about. Rupert Merson plugs the gap
with another of his insightful, irreverent, but as always informative guides.

ISBN 1 86197 682 8

£6.99

An Inspector Returns
The A–Z to surviving a tax investigation
by Daniel Dover & Tim Hindle
with cartoons by Michael Heath

Revised and updated second edition

If you are the subject of a tax investigation by the Inland Revenue, do not panic – read this book instead. An investigation undoubtedly means trouble, but the straightforward advice in these pages should help steer you around the worst pitfalls and survive the process intact.

'An amusing guide through this difficult subject ... This disarmingly honest little book could save you many sleepless nights.' *The Times*

ISBN 1 86197 420 5

£6.99

War or Peace
Skirmishes with the Revenue
by Daniel Dover & Tim Hindle
with cartoons by McLachlan

Each year over 250,000 people are subject to Inland Revenue enquiries. It is not a pleasant experience. But help is at hand. For the first time here is a book that explains the whole process, along with numerous tips on how to proceed and what to do – or not to do. Deftly written with wit and humour, this could save you time, misery and money.

'This is a terrific book … It is informative, easy to understand and comforting. Full marks.' *The Tax Journal*

ISBN 1 86197 524 4

£6.99